4/13
m

My First Pet Library from the American Humane Association

My First Cat

American Humane®

Protecting
Children & Animals
Since 1877

Enslow Elementary
an imprint of
Enslow Publishers, Inc.
40 Industrial Road
Box 398
Berkeley Heights, NJ 07922
USA

http://www.enslow.com

Linda Bozzo

American Humane.

Protecting
Children & Animals
Since 1877

Founded in 1877, the American Humane Association is the oldest national organization dedicated to protecting both children and animals. Through a network of child and animal protection agencies and individuals, the American Humane Association develops policies, legislation, curricula, and training programs to protect children and animals from abuse, neglect, and exploitation. To learn how you can support the vision of a nation where no child or animal will ever be a victim of willful abuse or neglect, visit www.americanhumane.org, phone (303) 792-9900, or write to the American Humane Association at 63 Inverness Drive East, Englewood, Colorado, 80112-5117.

This book is dedicated to my husband and daughters, who never stop believing in me, and to pet lovers everywhere.

Library of Congress Cataloging-in-Publication Data

Bozzo, Linda.
   My first cat / Linda Bozzo.
      p. cm. — (My first pet library from the American Humane Association)
   Includes bibliographical references and index.
   ISBN-13: 978-0-7660-2750-3
   ISBN-10: 0-7660-2750-3
      1. Cats—Juvenile literature. I. Title.
   II. Series: Bozzo, Linda. My first pet library from the American Humane Association.
   SF447.B65 2007
   636.8—dc22   2006008403

Printed in the United States of America
042010 Lake Book Manufacturing, Inc. Melrose Park, IL

10 9 8 7 6 5 4

To Our Readers: We have done our best to make sure all Internet Addresses in this book were active and appropriate when we went to press. However, the author and the publisher have no control over and assume no liability for the material available on those Internet sites or on other Web sites they may link to. Any comments or suggestions can be sent by e-mail to comments@enslow.com or to the address on the back cover.

Every effort has been made to locate all copyright holders of material used in this book. If any errors or omissions have occurred, corrections will be made in future editions of this book.

Illustration Credits: © 1996–2004 ArtToday, Inc., p. 13; Comstock, pp. 12, 16, 16 (right), 19, 20; Corel Corporation, p. 15; Eyewire, p. 5; Richard Hutchings/PhotoEdit, p. 9; Michael Newman/PhotoEdit, p. 27; Painet Inc., p. 14; PhotoDisc, Inc., pp. 8, 10, 21, 31; © 2002 PIXTAL, p. 11; George Shelley/Masterfile, p. 3; Shutterstock, pp. 1, 4, 6, 7, 17 (left), 18, 22, 23, 24, 25, 26, 28.

Cover Credits: Brand X Pictures.

Contents

Purr-fect Pets

Cats make purr-fect pets. Watching them is fun. They like to climb. They like to jump. Cats also like to take naps and have time alone. Like all pets, your furry friend will need love and care. Choosing the right cat for you is important.

This book can help answer questions you may have about finding and caring for your new pet cat.

Some cats like to be held like this. There are many ways to hold a cat.

What Kind of Cat Do I Want?

There are many kinds of cats.

Some have long hair. Some have short hair.

Cats come in many sizes and colors.

They all make good pets.

Cats like to play. You can buy special cat toys at a pet store.

Some cats
have short
hair.

Some cats have long hair.

A great place to get a cat is from an **animal shelter**. Animal shelters are full of cats that need a good home. Some people **adopt** cats from friends or neighbors. You can also adopt a cat from a rescue group. Rescue groups save animals and make sure they go to good homes.

Kittens are fun to play with, but be gentle!

Pick a healthy cat with
bright, clear eyes. Make
sure the cat has a dry
nose. A healthy cat
has clean ears
and teeth.

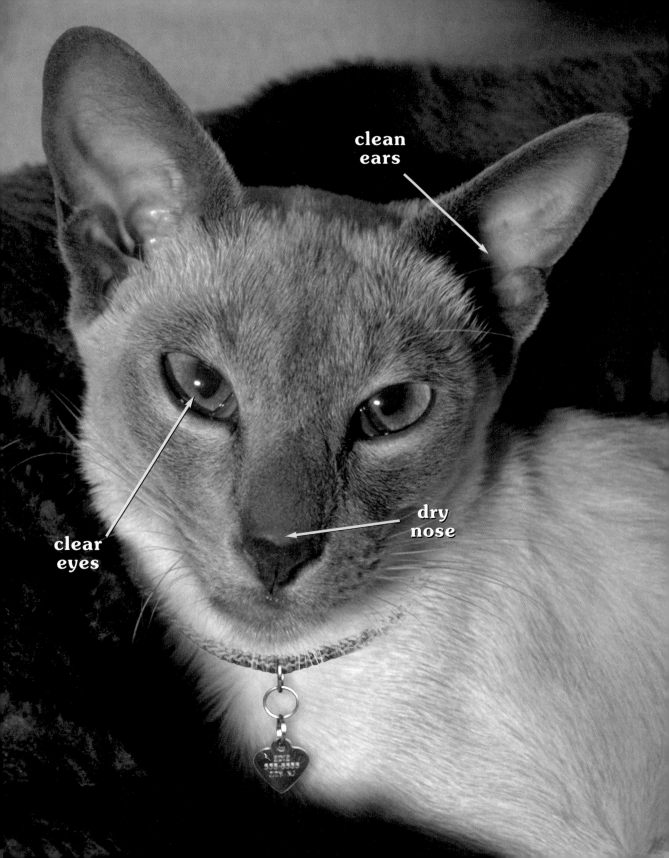

clean
ears

clear
eyes

dry
nose

What Will My Cat Need?

Every cat needs a warm, safe place to curl up. For sleeping, your cat might like a cozy bed.

Your cat should have his own food and water dishes. Keep the dishes clean.

Your cat will need a litter box. This is the cat's bathroom. Clean the litter every day. Empty the box and wash it once a week.

Your new cat should have a collar with a tag. If your cat gets lost, the tag will help her get returned safely.

The tag should have your:

- Cat's name
- Family's name
- Address
- Phone number

"Scooter"
The Devon Family
97 Main St.
Old Town, PA
(123) 555-9876

Ask your vet about putting a **microchip** under your cat's skin.

Cats need to scratch to keep their nails sharp. Place a scratching post in your cat's favorite room. Train him to use the scratching post so he won't scratch your furniture.

scratching post

Cats like to play. Keep your cat happy with toys. Playing with your cat will let her run around.

It is best to use a carrier when you take your cat places. A carrier is a special box with air holes and a door. It is a safe way to take your cat when you go places.

carrier

How Can I Keep My Cat Healthy?

You will want to take your cat to a **vet**, or animal doctor, for checkups. The vet can help keep your cat healthy.

Just like people, cats need shots to protect them from illness. These shots are called **vaccinations**.

Bring your new pets to the vet right away. The vet will make sure they are healthy.

18

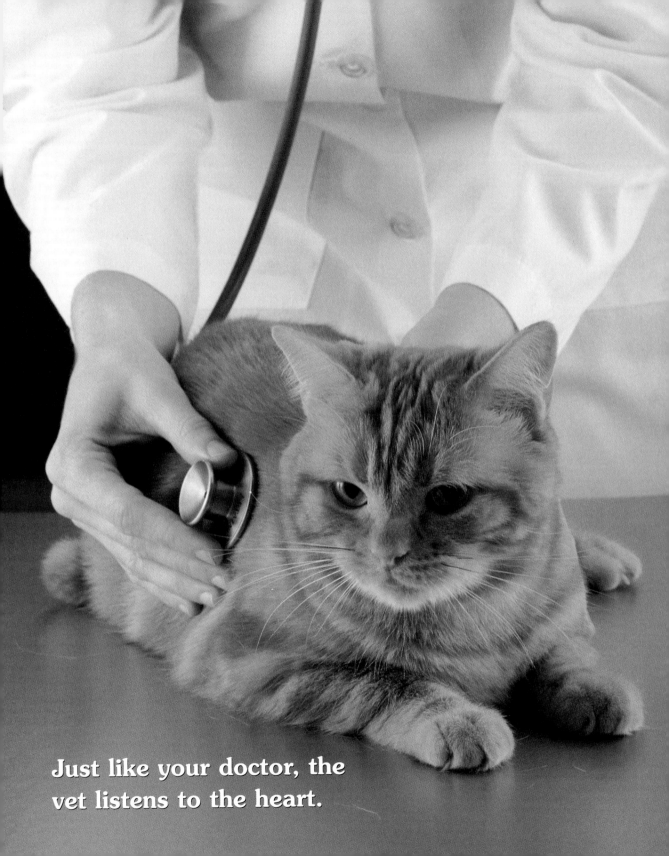

Just like your doctor, the vet listens to the heart.

If you like animals, you can be a vet.

Spaying and **neutering** are operations that cats get so they cannot have unwanted kittens. These operations can also help cats stay healthy.

For the safety and health of your cat, it is also best to keep your cat indoors.

Ask your vet if you have any questions about caring for your new pet.

What Should I Feed My Cat?

Feed your cat a good cat food. The vet can tell you what food is best for your cat.

Cats should also have fresh, cool water to drink.

Make sure your new pet has fresh water. Check it often. Refill his bowl if he needs more.

Will I Need to Give My Cat a Bath?

Cats almost never need baths. They clean themselves with their tongues. Sometimes cats will get hair in their stomachs. This can cause hair balls, which can make your cat sick.

Cats use their rough tongues to clean themselves.

Brush your cat often with a special brush.

You will want to brush or comb your cat often. This will help keep your cat from getting hair balls. It will also mean less hair around your house.

Give your new cat time to get used to you. Soon your cat will have a special place in your home. With lots of love and care, your furry friend will live a long and healthy life with you.

Your cat can live a long time and will be a good friend.

Words to Know

adopt—To take an animal into your home.

animal shelter—A place where animals that need homes are kept.

microchip—A small computer chip. It can be put under a cat's skin. If your cat gets lost, the microchip can be scanned by a special computer. This will show who owns the cat.

neutering—An operation male cats have so they cannot have kittens.

spaying—An operation female cats have so they cannot have kittens.

vaccinations—Shots that a cat needs to protect against illness.

vet—Vet is short for veterinarian, a doctor who takes care of animals.

Read About

BOOKS

Frost, Helen. *Cats.* Mankato, Minn.: Pebble Books, 2001.

Gillis, Jennifer Blizin. *Cats.* Chicago, Ill.: Heinemann Library, 2004.

Holub, Joan. *Why Do Cats Meow?* New York: Dial Books for Young Readers, 2001.

Rayner, Matthew. *Cat.* Milwaukee, Wisc.: Gareth Stevens Pub., 2004.

Simon, Seymour. *Cats.* New York: HarperCollins Publishers, 2004.

Walker, Niki, and Bobbie Kalman. *Kittens.* New York: Crabtree Pub. Co., 2004.

INTERNET ADDRESSES

American Humane Association
<http://www.americanhumane.org>
Learn more about animals at this Web site.

The Cat Fanciers' Association, Inc.
<http://www.cfainc.org/caring.html>
Find out more about different cat breeds.

Index